DISCA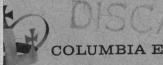

COLLEGE OF SAN MATEO LIBRARY

D1179963

COLUMBIA ESSA S

NUMBER CE $.65

JEAN GENET

by Tom F. Driver

65/N

Jean Genet

by TOM F. DRIVER

Columbia University Press

NEW YORK & LONDON 1966

LIBRARY — COLLEGE OF SAN MATEO

COLUMBIA ESSAYS ON MODERN WRITERS is a series of critical studies of English, Continental, and other writers whose works are of contemporary artistic and intellectual significance.

Editor: William York Tindall

Advisory Editors
Jacques Barzun   W. T. H. Jackson   Joseph A. Mazzeo   Justin O'Brien

Jean Genet is Number 20 of the series

TOM F. DRIVER, Associate Professor of Christian Theology, at Union Theological Seminary in New York, is the author of *The Sense of History in Greek and Shakespearean Drama.*

Copyright © 1966 Columbia University Press
Library of Congress Catalog Card Number: 66-26003
Printed in the United States of America

Passages from the following works of Jean Genet are quoted by permission of Grove Press, Inc.: *The Thief's Journal,* translated from the French by Bernard Frechtman, copyright © 1964 by Jean Genet; *The Balcony,* translated from the French by Bernard Frechtman, copyright © 1958, 1960, by Bernard Frechtman. Passages from *Querelle de Brest,* by Jean Genet, copyright © 1953 by Editions Gallimard, are quoted by permission of Editions Gallimard.

60092

Jean Genet

"I was born in Paris on December 19, 1910. As a ward of the *Assistance Publique*, it was impossible for me to know anything about my background. When I was twenty-one, I obtained a birth certificate. My mother's name was Gabrielle Genet. My father remains unknown."

Such is the way Genet describes his accident of birth, but his project in life has been to transform accident into necessity. Cast off at birth, he came to love those who are rejected and who reject each other. He sought the company of those whose love, though passionate, is false, because it is founded on betrayal. This contradiction he made his reality.

Genet was placed as a foster child in the home of peasants in the mountains of Burgundy. No ties, whether of love or hatred, seem to have been established between him and this family. At an early age he began to steal, and while he was still a child he was sent to a reformatory known as the Colonie de Mettray. There his identification with the world of the condemned was fixed.

It would be too simple, and unfair to Genet's own testimony, to blame his anti-social behavior upon any abuses of justice suffered at the Colonie. The more just his punishers, the more Genet affirmed them in their punitive roles, for this meant a corresponding affirmation of himself as one who deserved to be punished and whose punishment defined his nature.

Released from Mettray, Genet entered upon a life of vagabondage and thievery which carried him over much of the

European continent and into the prisons of many countries. He stole cattle in Albania, was a pickpocket in Venice, smuggled narcotics, started a black-market in Berlin, joined and deserted the French Foreign Legion, lived as a thief in most of the ports along the Atlantic and Mediterranean. "The police of the various European countries," he wrote, "inspired me with fear, just as they do any other thief." However, he preferred the police of France. "The French police moved me . . . through a kind of terror, the source of which was in my feeling of native and irrevocable guilt." He has also said, "What I committed outside of France was not sin but an error." He explained his return to France after a long absence by saying, "Perhaps I wanted to accuse myself in my own language."

In France Genet was locked up at various times in the Maison Centrale at Fontrevault, La Santé and Prison des Tourelles at Paris, and the prison at Fresnes. It was at Fresnes that he began to write. There, in 1942, he completed his first book, *Notre-Dame-des-Fleurs*. There he also wrote, perhaps first, a long, incantatory poem called "Le Condamné à mort," dedicated to his friend and fellow criminal, Maurice Pilorge, who had been executed the seventeenth of March, 1939.

By the year 1948 Genet was the author of three published novels (*Notre-Dame-des-Fleurs, Miracle de la rose, and Pompes funèbres*), two published plays (*Les Bonnes* and *Haute surveillance*), and two long poems published together as *Chants secrets*. He was in prison, sentenced for life at his tenth conviction for theft. The most prominent literary figures of France petitioned for his release. Their number included Paul Claudel, François Mauriac, André Gide, Jean-Paul Sartre, and Jean Cocteau. Pardon was granted by Vincent Auriol, then President of the French Republic. The period of Genet's official condemnation was over. Faced with an inner crisis occasioned by liberty and fame, Genet wrote no more for six years, though what he had already written was widely dis-

[4]

cussed. He became the subject of a mammoth work (*Saint Genet*) written by Jean-Paul Sartre. The eminent publishing house, Gallimard, began to issue his *Oeuvres complètes*, of which the work by Sartre became, oddly, Volume I. Then in 1956 Genet brought forth a new play, *Le Balcon*. His dramatic power continued to grow in *Les Nègres* (1958) and *Les Paravents* (1961). A film, *Mademoiselle*, for which Genet wrote the screenplay, directed by Tony Richardson and starring Jeanne Moreau, was released in the summer of 1966. Genet avoids contact with the press and the literary world as much as possible. It is his nature, and part of his literary gift, to attack or else to scorn his audience. What can one say of the literary accomplishment of such a figure?

In any account of the works written by Jean Genet, as well as in any assessment of them, it is necessary to take full cognizance of their language of sexuality. Genet is a pornographer. Yet his attitude toward pornographic detail is different from that of most persons, and in literature there is nothing quite like it. Genet does not introduce descriptions of sexual acts and desires in order to achieve a Zolaesque realism or to add spice to his pages or to gain a humorous effect. He does not use sex primarily to shock the reader or to incur the wrath of censors. (In America, where *Fanny Hill*, *Lady Chatterley's Lover*, and *Tropic of Cancer* have landed in the courts, Genet's work has provoked no censorship proceedings, although his movie, *Chant d'amour*, has been suppressed.) The sex in Genet's writing is there for one reason only: because it is the starting point for everything else, and the point to which all returns. Could one say the same of *Fanny Hill?* No, for there is almost nothing else *in* Cleland's book, no other order of experience illuminated by the sexual. By contrast, Genet is a *serious* pornographer. One thinks of comparing him with de Sade. The Marquis de Sade, however, leaves one with the

[5]

impression that his mind and spirit have been possessed by a certain kind of sexuality, whereas Genet is no more obsessed with sex than was Freud. He has simply observed that his behavior and his imagination are functions of his sexuality, and apart from it cannot be expressed. "The word balls [*couilles*]," he writes, "is a roundness in my mouth. I am aware that my gravity, when I invent this part of the body, becomes my most essential virtue. Just as the magician draws countless wonders from his hat, I can draw from them all the other virtues."

The use of perverse sexuality to which Genet aspired in his writing and to which he attained is of a mythopoeic kind. It structures and renders available to consciousness the meaningful world. The raw sensual data are fed to the conscience and "located" with regard to the self by the will. They enter into a dialectical formation with the intelligence. The end result is a metaphysics, a "world," and in some of the works a structure so nearly perfect that it will certainly endure the hostility of time.

The sexual myth is unambiguously present in Genet's earliest writing, the poem "Le Condamné à mort" ("The One Condemned to Death"), but there it is so crude that a reader might wonder how it could ever produce anything of value. The poet's young lover, an assassin, has been sentenced to die. This gives him, in the poet's eye, a glory he could not otherwise possess. He becomes the image of the ideal killer, full of masculine power, and all the more attractive because, as a killer, he is going to be killed. Genet recalls the intimacies of their prison nights; but he is no master of verse, and "Le Condamné à mort" is full of juvenile conceits. It ends with the apotheosis of the executed criminal, who is addressed as God, Lord, Hermes of the tender foot, and Jesus. The relation between the resurrected "Jesus" and his supplicant is graphically sexual, deliberately indecent.

[6]

The trouble here is not the indecency, which Genet will never abandon, but the fact that the materials which belong to Genet's myth of perverse sexuality are here nothing but raw images. In order to function properly they will have to become part of a narrative. Not the image of death but the myth of the dying king will provide Genet's better works with their extraordinary power. Why the myth of the dying king and that of perverse sexuality are virtually the same is something we shall have to discover.

We do not know the dates of composition of Genet's other poems. "Marche funèbre," published together with "Le Condamné à mort" in 1945, is likewise addressed to the condemned youth, Pilorge. As it is a somewhat better poem (actually a series of related ones), it must have been written after the other. "La Galère" invokes the memory of another condemned murderer, Harcamone, whom Genet knew at the prison at Fontrevault. "La Parade" consists of three short prison meditations, two of them about the deaths of children. "Un chant d'amour" is dedicated to Lucien Sénemaud, another of Genet's lovers. "Le pêcheur du Suquet" is the best of the poems, partly because much of it is in prose and because it is more fully dramatized than the others. On the whole, Genet's poetry is disappointing. His talent requires the larger spaces of the novel and the drama, which, as it turned out, he was able to use with exceptional ability.

Notre-Dame-des-Fleurs (*Our Lady of the Flowers*), dated 1942 at the Prison de Fresnes, is a book of extreme, one wants to say dizzying, complexity, though its plot, as Joseph H. McMahon has pointed out, is actually quite simple. Louis Culafroy, who, like Genet, spent his childhood in the provinces, becomes a male prostitute in Paris. He changes his name to Divine and his sexual (not his physical) identity from masculine to feminine. He undergoes an emotional disintegration, first through the pain of losing a number of lovers, and second through jealousy of a more attractive youth, Adrien Baillou, known as Notre-Dame-des-Fleurs. Our Lady, whose beauty moves even the court before which he is tried, confesses to a murder and is sentenced. Divine dies of tuberculosis.

If the story is simple, its telling is not. For instance, Genet employs the feminine pronoun "she" when referring to some, though not all, of his male characters. A few women actually appear in the narrative, notably Divine's mother. Essentially, however, the world of this novel is one in which only males exist. This masculine subworld, the only place where anything *happens*, is subdivided into the masculine and the feminine. The prostitutes and other dependent types are "she." The "toughs," the dominant types who plan the daring escapades of theft and sometimes murder, are "he." This division is a mockery of the "normal" world, on which it depends for its terminology and some of its conventions, and which it also derides.

The society shown is the anti-type of the "normal." In it there is a "necessary" conjunction of love and violence, which psychology leads us to anticipate because of the sado-masochistic element in homosexuality. What interests Genet, however, is not the psychology, which he takes for granted, but something more nearly philosophical, namely, the inversion of the "normal." Violence belongs, at some level, to heterosexual love. If we are not aware of it, Genet will make us so. Usually, however, we regard the violent component of love as its minor part, subordinated to tenderness, affection, and regard for the partner's welfare. Genet inverts this. Violence becomes the essence of the relationship, its major component. Tenderness, joy, affection, the regard for the other's well-being become subordinate elements which do no more than flavor an affair and sometimes render it poignant. They never belong to its substance. In anti-society love becomes anti-love, which is not the same as hatred (though Genet has said that he finds tenderness in hatred) and certainly not the same as lack of passion.

[8]

The scenes of *Notre-Dame-des-Fleurs* move through time and space with a freedom that appears at first nearly chaotic. Actually, this movement is the opposite of chaos. It is very firmly controlled. It is determined, however, not by the logic of narrative and not by any schematic treatment of time as was employed, for instance, by William Faulkner in *The Sound and the Fury*, but by a principle of association. An incident, a remark, a gesture, or an object will recall a similar (or contrasting) figure of another place and time. Within the paragraph, or even the sentence, a shift of scene will accordingly be made. The effect is that of a cinematic "dissolve." Following a single, perhaps slender, linkage, the reader must begin to think himself into a new scene, only to be dislocated again in a short time. In this manner a single scene can be built up of many layers, like transparencies laid one upon the other; when we return to a scene after several "dissolves" into others, all linked by associated figures, we carry all the ancillary scenes in our mind as layered meanings of the main one. However, since what is now a secondary scene may later become primary, reversing the relations of dominance and subordinance, the total effect is of an enormous complexity which is at the same time highly compact. There is something of Proust in this method, though the spirit and style are different. There is also something child-like in the method: correspondences of similar things remote in space and time tend to cancel out their respective historical contexts. Moreover, the method is one which deliberately creates frustration. In Genet's world, one is never at rest. Scenes do not end; before they are over they spawn other scenes. Affairs do not end; they dissolve into other affairs. And sexual embraces, of which there are many, each longed for with an intense burden of desire, are, in their occurrence, physically voluptuous and psychologically anticlimactic. Genet's pornography is *true* pornography; it reveals with astounding candor the hunger which the pornographic imagination stimulates but cannot feed.

[9]

Because of its shifts in time and space, because each of its characters is in some sense a mask for every other, and because the totality of the "world" it constructs is an inversion of the reader's world, *Notre-Dame-des-Fleurs* whirls in one's consciousness. Yet its whirling is somehow located, as if firmly oriented round a center that is present but is not expressed. Its centrifugal tendencies are balanced by an equally strong centripetal pull. One feels that the work moves in a perfectly regular and unchanging orbit. What pulls it to the center? And what *is* the center?

The center is Genet, writing the book, as he explains, alone in his prison cell. Its characters are drawn from his memories of various lovers, prostitutes, pimps, thieves, and murderers. Yet what we read is not autobiography but memory turned into fiction and fiction turned into fantasy, for the idea of the book is that the solitary prisoner brings before his mind's eye those figures, those intrigues, and those conceits of fancy that will stimulate his desire, in order that he may bring himself to orgasm. *Notre-Dame-des-Fleurs* is made of the fantasies of an onanist. It records the desires of a homosexual who intends to masturbate while thinking of the most beautiful boys and most formidable "toughs" he has known.

This, however, is only the most obvious and least important sense in which Genet is at the center of *Notre-Dame-des-Fleurs*. By itself it can only explain why the book is bizarre. It cannot explain why it interests those who do not share its lusts and who have little curiosity about Genet's kind of psychosexual pathology. The deeper sense in which Genet is at the center of his book is that he participates in its central myth, which is that of the dying king. This myth is not directly expressed in the book, but its presence is everywhere felt.

In actual fact, the Genet who writes *Notre-Dame-des-Fleurs* is a nobody, even in the underworld he glorifies. In imagination, he is sovereign. There he may rule over all the characters he recalls. There he makes them subject to his wishes by transforming them into ideal forms. For this purpose he can use, in addition to his memories, the faces of unknown criminals and athletes whose pictures he has cut from newspapers and glued to the wall of his cell.

Thus with the aid of my unknown lovers I am going to write a story. My heroes are those there pasted to the wall, those and I who am there, coupled with them. In the degree and measure that you will read, the characters, and Divine also, and Culafroy, will fall from the wall onto my pages like dead leaves in order to fertilize my narrative.

The characters of this whirling book move as in a dance. The work is, in fact, a "masque of blackness." It is a ceremony of the imagination. The "royal" figure for whom it is performed is Genet himself, its creator and its ideal spectator. This king is dying. Projecting himself narcissistically into the person of Adrien Baillou, who is transformed into Our Lady of the Flowers, a queen of heaven, he achieves his greatest moment when he confesses to a motiveless murder and is condemned as if he were a tragic king. As Louis Culafroy, called Divine, Genet becomes another queen who bears a sacred name. This queen of a society unrecognized by ordinary mortals is tawdry and pathetic. So much the better for her secret glory. Her life is not a series of events but a sequence of rites. Hers is a secret ceremony put on by and for a secret king, who is also secretly a queen, holding lavish court with a clandestine retinue. The magic of it makes Genet shudder. It is all a matter of transformations, masks, epiphanies. As such it is of a sweetness not even the touch of flesh can equal.

The secret ritual can have no other end but death. "Their death, will I need to tell you of that?" he asks, referring to all of his characters. The words that introduce Divine tell us that she "died yesterday in a pool of blood" like the blood

[11]

of Jesus or of someone assassinated. All the characters, says Genet, will have the death "of the one who, when he learned of his own from the jury, was content to murmur . . . 'I am already further along than that.' " The king must die. The king's subjects, being royal, must also die. Their life *is* their dying, and their dying is their life. Fate is their only reality.

All this is of imagination, the mind playing with itself. From imagining to writing, there is a step to be taken. One may say that Genet became a writer because of the seriousness with which he took his role as imaginary king. He knew that to be king is more than to have subjects, to preside at ceremonies, and to die. A king must also govern. Genet began to write because he began to desire to govern the figures of his imagination. He began to wish to control the terrain of language, within which alone the creatures of his memory and of his transforming fantasy might have a life not identical with his own yet not really independent either, a life of sufficient objectivity and otherness as to acquire substance and therefore the need to be ruled by a sovereign's power. For Genet, writing is the extended realization of the dialectic implied in king and subject. This is a very different dialectic from that implied, for instance, in the terms writer and reader. The difference is important for the understanding of all the books and plays that he has written.

When Genet enacts in himself the myth of the dying king, he does so pre-eminently in his function as writer. He has made himself, at least in his own mind, the archetype of the writer as monarch of his own creation. This accounts for the reader's feeling of being in the presence of something absolute when he approaches Genet's works. In them there may be much fantasy; there is nothing accidental. The monarch may rule over an impending chaos, but he rules. He faces death from two causes. He may die slowly of exhaustion, worn out by the sheer effort, which can never relax, to subordinate creativity to order. And if he succeeds in his ideal of sovereignty, he will have achieved that perfect order which is the same as spiritual death.

Genet is therefore a king who is *fated* to die. Nevertheless, by his acute awareness of this destiny, he is "already further along than that." Like the Christ of some theologies, he fulfills the destiny to which he is bound while he stands outside of it and watches. Genet's destiny, however, does not bring any salvation. On the contrary, its function is to bring all Messianic expectation to a halt and to effect a magical, illusory, and awesome transformation of good into evil. This is the "impossible possibility" which Genet has willed for his compulsive kingdom. It haunts and troubles all men of letters because it tends to summon up what Wallace Fowlie has called "the latent suspicion in all of us that literature is not innocent but guilty." Perhaps it also suggests that *man* is not innocent, that his imagination is inherently diabolic.

After *Notre-Dame-des-Fleurs*, Genet wrote *Miracle de la rose*. Dated 1943 at the Prison des Tourelles and La Santé, it has the same fluid structure as *Notre-Dame* and produces a similar whirling effect; but it is less dizzying because it seems (perhaps this is deceptive) closer to fact and because it has only two settings, the prison at Fontrevault and the reformatory at Metray. It is not a novel but an autobiographical meditation, which is also true of *Pompes funèbres* (*Funeral Pomp*) and *Journal du voleur* (*The Thief's Journal.*)

There are four principal characters: Divers, who has been Genet's lover some fifteen years before at Mettray; the young Bulkaen, with whom Genet falls deeply in love; Harcamone, who is sentenced to die for killing a guard; and Genet himself, whose passions are the subject of the book. The evocations of prison life, both at Fontrevault and at Mettray, are of an extraordinary, compelling vividness.

[13]

The book is built upon a system of degrees of reality, as in a kind of dark Platonism. For instance, there is a hierarchy of evil and power which reaches its acme in Harcamone; yet this zenith is actually a nadir, for Harcamone is incarcerated alone in a cell in the depths of the prison.

Finally Fontrevault burns also (but with a pale light, very sweet) from the illuminations which Harcamone, the condemned to death, sends out from its blackest heart, its secret hiding places.

Leaving la Santé for Fontrevault, I knew already that Harcamone was waiting there for his execution. At my arrival, I was therefore seized by the mystery of one of my former comrades at Mettray, who had known how to push the adventure common to all of us to its most extreme point: that death on the scaffold which is our glory. Harcamone had "succeeded." And this success, not being of the terrestrial order, like fortune or honor, provoked in me astonishment and admiration in the face of the accomplished thing (even the most simple is miraculous) but also the fear which upsets one who witnesses a magical operation.

There is also a hierarchy of beauty. The young criminal Bulkaen is at its top, though Genet is aware that Bulkaen's beauty may be the result of another "magical operation" performed on the boy's ordinary appearances by Genet's love. There is a hierarchy of guilt, in which more is better, and according to which Mettray is romanticized as the place where childhood innocence was lost. The climax of the book is reached when Genet incurs his greatest guilt by betraying Harcamone, already the supremely guilty one. Genet had vowed to keep a vigil, to watch and wait until the hour of Harcamone's death. But when Divers wants to make love to Genet on the very night of execution, Genet abandons himself to sensual pleasures, partly to compensate for the loss of Bulkaen, who is dead, and partly in order to "betray" Harcamone and thus to reach in his own cowardly way a state of abjection and guilt that may increase his affinity with the "saintly" criminal in his hour of agony.

In this world of Platonic levels and participations, all is in-

[14]

verted. Lower is higher, perseverance in evil is the way of sain
liness, betrayal is devotion, and the mask is more nearly re
than what it covers. It is precisely the falseness of it all th
stirs Genet's passion, yet in some ways reality itself seen
party to his deceptions. The prison at Fontrevault is a forme
abbey. Those who now walk its corridors, occupy its littl
cells, wear homespun garments and exist in poverty, divorce
from the world, living by the "rule" of their superiors, boun
together by common values and honoring certain mysterie
—these are the "monks" of this place. They are the inheritor
of the sacred aura which belongs to the very name of Fontrevault, and though their mysteries are the opposite of their
predecessors', nevertheless they belong to the same reality and
are its most nearly complete expression.

Let no one be surprised if the images which indicate my movement
are the opposite of those which indicate the movement of the saints
of heaven. One will say of them that they ascend, and of me that I
degrade myself.

So it is that I traverse the tortuous ways which are, to tell the
truth, the same paths for my heart and for sanctity.

Benjamin Nelson has said that Sartre's book, *Saint Genet,*
must be interpreted as a kind of hagiography. The same is to
be observed of Genet's *Miracle de la rose,* a devotional book in
which criminals and condemned men are treated as saints in
order that their numinous reality may find its way into the
being of Genet, who is already king of an imaginary realm
and wishes now, like kings of old, to enter upon a pilgrimage.

Harcamone is dead. Bulkaen is dead. If I go out, as after the death
of Pilorge, I will leaf through old newspapers. As with Pilorge,
there will remain between my hands only a very brief article, on
cheap paper, a sort of gray ash which will tell me that he was
executed at dawn. These papers are their tomb. But I will send their
name very far into time. This name, alone, will remain in the
future, rid of its object. Who were Bulkaen, Harcamone, Divers,
who was Pilorge, who was Guy? someone will ask. And their
name will be troublesome as the light troubles us which arrives

from a star that died a thousand years ago. . . . I am silent and go on walking barefoot.

The mood, and also the motif, of *Miracle de la rose* is surrender—surrender to love, to destiny, to manifestations of holiness as evil, to degradation, and so on. Before the miracle of transformation, the devout man humbles himself, knowing that in surrender he will find his glory. This fact makes *Miracle de la rose* easily read as an analogue of more "normal" religious and aesthetic experiences, in which light many readers will see it as the most beautiful of Genet's books, a designation which Sartre has reserved for *The Thief's Journal*.

One thinks of surrender when one feels the presence of an overwhelming power. When such power manifests itself indirectly, as through exceptional beauty or through miracle, the awe that it occasions may be admirable; the fear of the Lord is the beginning of wisdom, as the psalmist has it. When, however, power manifests itself directly as nothing other than superior force, any surrender it may occasion is not admirable but signifies mere weakness, or cowardice, or both. *Miracle de la rose*, although it includes, as all Genet's works do, many references to the direct show of power, is given its particular tone and symbolic organization by the fact that its main concern is the indirect manifestation of power. The author maintains a religious reticence to declare the name of his Holy One or to describe his face. Instead, he dwells on the "divine" attributes and on the "saintliness" of the various males who participate in the "divine" substance. The book describes the ascetic "way" which Genet, as true believer, must follow, knowing with some despair that he can never attain to the high estate of those who, like Harcamone, emit a tragic, evil, and holy radiance.

In his next book, *Pompes funèbres* (*Funeral Pomp*, published in 1947), Genet attempted a more audacious feat. He tried

[16]

to express the motif of surrender by describing his capitulation before manifestations of power that were direct. A number of critics have called the result a total failure. It demonstrates how disastrous direct statement can be for an artist whose basic concerns are psychological and mystical. It also shows that at this stage of his development Genet's *bête noire* was history. In spite of the fact that some passages in the book are as well written as any Genet has composed, it is virtually impossible to forgive Genet for having appropriated the misery of millions to his own psychological needs.

That the extraordinary show of naked and arbitrary power in Hitler's Germany should prove congenial to Genet's particular sort of homosexual vision is perhaps not surprising, since both contained a great deal of sado-masochism, glorified the act of killing, exalted the young male, and were "sublimely" destructive. Naziism was conceived of as a glorification of violence, was attended by pseudo-mythology of a compensatory nature and was destined to be destroyed by violence, as Genet's murderers are destined to reach their glory on the scaffold. How could Genet, who already hated France yet preferred to accuse himself in the French language, fail to perceive that the most "beautiful" political act he could perform would be to betray that nation by collaborating with her conquerors, in whose arms he would find a refuge from his own weakness and from all that was "good"? The double risk of it—that he might be killed either by those he betrayed or by the cruel ones whose protection he sought—only added to its allure and the sense of its fatal necessity.

All this is not surprising as part of Genet's psychology and his affirmation of the ontological supremacy of evil. The only surprising thing is that he actually wrote and published a book in which Hitler is praised as the ultimate manifestation of power; in which Genet is first the lover of a Communist member of the Resistance (who is killed in street fighting in August,

[17]

1944) and a few days later takes as lover a member of the Waffen SS; in which Genet imagines himself the fearful yet happy object of the amorous advances of a huge man called "the hangman of Berlin." All this and much more in the book are sheer adoration of power, combined with dreams of masochistic pleasure.

Joseph H. McMahon has pointed out that *Pompes funèbres* contains in very clear form a certain "ethic," characteristic of all Genet's writing, which may be seen to have three cardinal principles. First, evil is its own vindication, provided it is willed and not entered upon by mere accident. Second, there is a cycle in human affairs which moves first one man and then another into a position of supreme power. The high point one may reach on this wheel of fortune is the possession and use of power, which may also be called virility. From the top, one must descend toward destruction. Third, and perhaps most important, within the cycle there occur certain transferences of power. The man on top initiates his successor into the fraternity of evil power through an act of humiliation, usually sexual. The transference of power thus begun leads the neophyte to the top of the heap, after which a new transference takes place.

In such a view, power is eternal, though its bearers or exemplars are mortal. Their glory is to have participated in a dynamic process that creates, exalts, and destroys them. Virtue is not an attribute of individuals, and the pursuit of virtue is incompatible with fidelity to persons. Instead, it requires one's allegiance to change when power shifts from one bearer to another. When Genet's affections move from Jean, the slain Resistance fighter, to Erik, the SS man who may have been responsible for Jean's death, there is "betrayal" only in "our" sense; for in Genet's "ethic" it is possible to adore in Erik a more excellent form of the virtue formerly admired in Jean. Such is the strange use of Platonic ideas, deliberately mutilated,

[18]

in *Pompes funèbres*. There could hardly be a more "sublime" justification of homosexual cowardice.

In the novel *Querelle de Brest* (published in 1947) Genet attempted to create a protagonist whose search for identity, self-understanding, and liberation would express in fictional terms a quest Genet himself had been following:

Little by little we recognized Querelle—already inside our flesh— grow and develop in our soul. . . . After this discovery of Querelle we want him to become the very type of the scorner. Following his destiny, his development, in ourself, we will see how it comes to be realized in a conclusion which seems to be . . . his own wish and his own destiny.

As a matter of fact, all the characters in *Querelle de Brest* are projections of various aspects of the author, just as in *Notre-Dame-des-Fleurs* each character is a mask for all the others. Querelle is the center of the work because in him Genet gathers up the conflicting tendencies of the other characters and shows how they are resolved in "this ideal and heroic personage, the fruit of our secret loves."

Querelle is a sailor from one of the ships in the port city of Brest. There is more than one murder in his past, and soon after the novel begins he commits another. As in *Pompes funèbres*, an important motif of the novel is the transference of power within a closed circle of characters. These include a ship's officer, Lieutenant Seblon, secretly in love with Querelle; Mario, the Chief of Police; Madame Lysiane, keeper of a brothel called La Féria; Nono, her husband; Robert, Querelle's brother; and various other sailors, workmen, and petty thieves. In every instance the power relationships are expressed by sexual relations, which means that the novel is made up of a fantastic series of scenes showing who does what to whom and why. The greatest variety is experienced by Querelle, for he discovers that if he gives himself to acts he had previously considered humiliating, and which indeed *are*, he may nevertheless retain and increase his independence by refusing to love, and by betraying those who trust and love him. This places him, as it were, outside the network of power transferences in which he appears to participate and enables him to use its energies for his own purposes. He is indeed the very type of the scorner, and there is nothing of which he is not capable.

As Querelle, in a kind of absolute though empty freedom, transcends the situations of which he is a part, so Genet transcends the novel which nevertheless proceeds wholly out of himself. This introduces the second, and even more important motif of the work, which is that of the relation of the creatures of imagination to their creator; and this, in turn, leads to what I have earlier called the myths of the dying king and of perverse sexuality.

Genet tells the reader that there are no pederasts in *Querelle de Brest* except Lieutenant Seblon. He, however, "is not *in* the book" because his desires are expressed only in a secret journal he keeps and not in his actions. Frequently the journal contains entries that seem to proceed from Genet as much as from the Lieutenant, as if the two have in common both the journal and the quality of being pederasts. At one point in the journal Genet/Seblon has expressed himself as follows:

Our intent is not to disengage two or more characters—or heroes, since they are drawn from a fabulous domain, that is to say, belonging to fable, to fable and to limbo—systematically odious. Rather let the reader desire to think that we are following an adventure which unfolds in ourself, in the deepest, the most unsocial part of our soul. Just so, it is because he animates his creatures—and voluntarily assumes the weight of the sin of this world born of himself—that the creator delivers, saves his creature, and in the same act places himself beyond or above the sin. May the reader escape the sin at the same time that, by his function and our word, he discovers these heroes in himself, insofar as they are already stagnating there.

In these words Genet declares himself as writer-creator-king and affirms that the function of such a being is god-like. His creation springs from the recesses of his own being, in particular from those parts that are the most odious and unacceptable to society. The one who fathers creatures from such a dark region knows that they are conceived in sin and that this sin is his own. Creating them is his act of expiation, not because he gets rid of his sin by loading it onto the characters but because, accepting *as his own* the full burden of the sin, he transcends it. The analogy with the sin-bearing of Christ is exact but is interpreted in psychological and existentialist terms. Freedom from guilt is achieved by the total acceptance of guilt, so that one's punisher and deliverer become one's self insofar as one is able to affirm (or accept) himself absolutely.

This idea is dramatized in a scene in which Querelle, having murdered a sailor, establishes himself in imagination as a "sovereign," arraigns himself, and condemns himself to death. The scene marks a crucial point in Querelle's movement toward freedom, his self authentication. Likewise, Seblon writes in his diary: "My vulgarity is royal and accords me all rights."

Genet invites the reader to accomplish, in his own regard, an act of self-awareness and self-acceptance similar to that which Genet as writer-king is accomplishing through his creation. He invites the reader to see, in the odious characters of the novel, figures that belong to his imagination but, inasmuch as they are unacknowledged and "forbidden," stagnate and are thus a source of corruption. The reader is offered the hope that, if he participates with Genet in the creative task of animating these figures, their corrupting power may be exorcised. Genet thus poses for every moral critic the question whether this offer of hope is itself authentic, or whether it is a form of seduction which, if accepted, would lead only toward a complicity in evil and an illusory freedom.

Insofar as Genet's appeal is to recognize the self's repressed sexual desires, to accept one's masculine and feminine duality, to accept the body and all its functions, and to dethrone all

[21]

merely bourgeois definitions of what is allowed, one may find oneself drawn by it for reasons not to be despised. Where one is faced with a very clear warning, however, is in the attitude Genet consistently maintains toward murder. It may be that in some spiritual sense we are all murderers, having intended this act on more than one occasion, and that the murders Genet describes can be read as paradigms of something already stagnant in our hearts. We must be careful, however, when we perceive that in Genet's eyes the actual result of a murder—the ending of a human life—is of no interest at all, while the sense of destiny that he imagines to attend the murderer's act is of an overwhelming immensity. It is the rigidity of this destiny, filling all the tissues of an otherwise flaccid life, that excites Genet and leads him to adore it with all the passion of a ravished soul. We come again to the myth of the dying king and the myth of perverse sexuality.

The ideal destiny of a mythical king is that he should die, and that not by accident but as the fulfillment of his royal nature. Thus his death proceeds from himself, even if it comes by another hand. The agent, in fact, is not important. What matters is that the king should die under his own condemnation. The criminal is revealed as a royal figure when, told he must die, he replies that he is "already further along than that." The criminal court, pitiful mockery that it is, can do no more than to ratify a judgment already made by the royal victim himself, can only do those things which fulfill what is already written. Bolingbroke is not interesting. It is Richard who knows and enacts his own destiny amid a glory of which Bolingbroke can never be aware.

The mention of Richard is enough, perhaps, to clue one to the overtones of sexual perversity which often accompany the myth of the dying king. Narcissism, sado-masochism, a hyperactive will and imagination combined with unusual passivity in practical matters, a compulsive attraction to ritual, and a tendency to take the sign for the substance—these are qualities that belong to Shakespeare's Richard, to Genet's heroes, and to the Genet who reveals himself in his style. Thus Genet tells us that his "ideal personage," Querelle, the "fruit of our secret loves," has in "his body, his attitudes, his exploits" an apparent beauty which is also real, and that the book is to show these in their "slow decomposition." The latter does not draw from Genet any cry of lament, since he never allows us to hear the voice of the tragic chorus. That would be a humanistic note. But here all is religious. All is as it should be. The king dies and, dying, is supreme. To be ravished by death is an eternal joy, comparable only to the sufferings the passive lover may sustain when he is entered by a superior and indifferent power.

The themes of *Journal du voleur* (*The Thief's Journal*, published in 1949), one of Genet's best and most widely admired books, are those of the previous works. Most of the events it describes took place in Spain, though parts of it also recall Antwerp, Paris, Marseilles, Czechoslovakia, Yugoslavia, and Germany. The life it recounts, Genet tells the reader, "was lived between 1932 and 1940." Like *Miracle de la rose*, this book is non-fiction; but that does not mean that what it describes is what actually happened, for Genet asserts that he does not write in order to re-create the past as it was but as it now lives in his mind. Experience is transformed into memory, and memory into words. The literary process, for Genet, is finding the right name for what is in consciousness. He tells us in *The Thief's Journal* that he has done this in his five books, and that therefore he will write no more. The theater was to reactivate Genet's desire to write, but he did not yet know this.

Although the motifs of *The Thief's Journal* are those of the earlier books, the naming surpasses them. The language of this work is of great clarity and precision. "My victory is verbal," says Genet, and he is right.

[23]

For instance, the motif of the creator-king is here given its most precise formulation:

Creating is not a somewhat frivolous game. The creator has committed himself to the fearful adventure of taking upon himself, to the very end, the perils risked by his creatures. . . . Jesus became man. He expiated. Later, like God, after creating men, He delivered them from their sins: He was whipped, spat upon, mocked, nailed. That is the meaning of the expression: "He suffers in the flesh." Let us ignore the theologians. "Taking upon Himself the sins of the world" means exactly this: experiencing potentially and in their effects all sins; it means having subscribed to evil. . . . We wish to regard this as one of the many uses of the generous myth of Creation and Redemption. Though the creator grants his characters free will, self-determination, he hopes, deep down in his heart, that they will choose Good. Every lover does likewise, hoping to be loved for his own sake.

The curious saintliness espoused by Genet, so similar to that of the saints of the Church and yet so different, is one in which the pursuit of evil and the awe of God are conjoined. "I shall impose a candid vision of evil," he says, "even though I lose my life, my honor, and my glory in this quest." Yet from blasphemy, the ultimate evil, he refrains:

I have been told that among the ancients Mercury was the god of thieves, who thus knew which power to invoke. But we have no one. It would seem logical to pray to the devil, but no thief would dare do so seriously. To make a compact with him would be to commit oneself too deeply. He is too opposed to God, Who, we know, is the final victor. A murderer himself would not dare pray to the devil.

Suspended between the ultimacy of God and the self-constructed fatality which binds him to evil, Genet exists nowhere, in a nothingness. Indeed, he calls *The Thief's Journal* a "pursuit of the Impossible Nothingness." It is no wonder that he imagined that when he had finished it there would be nothing else to write. To be sure, in its final paragraph he mentions a sequel (to be called *Morals Charge*) which will "comment upon the festivals of an inner prison I discover within me," but that inner prison had already been described.

[24]

There was, in fact, only one place Genet as writer could go, and that was to the theater. What it offered him of value was not an audience, although he got one, but rather that form of art which alone combines the two "unreal realities" upon which Genet's spiritual existence depends—the magic of words and the ritual of performance. His earlier works include many elements that must be understood in theatrical terms: the tendency to regard character as the mask of a hidden essence; the subsequent doubt as to whether this essence is real or only an illusion produced by the mask—that is, by the very idea of mask; the emphasis upon the beauty of an act, any act, provided it is complete, which means when it is taken as ritual, since it is only in ritual and not in real life that an act may properly be said to be complete; the delight taken in transformations, whereby a straight or mundane reality is clothed in the majesty of a symbolic representation; the acute sensitivity to the gestural quality of words, whereby the word in itself is a kind of act performed by the hidden being of things, and the gestures of men are already words; the dialectic of presentation, whereby a work of art consists of a motion which is the search for the ideal or supremely "right" expression of its own inner potentialities.

Genet's theater would have to be a ritual theater. It could not, like the theater of the boulevard, be the mere formalization of narrative into plot and intrigue. It would have to do with essences, fatalities, and magical transformations. His love of theater was, after all, born in him as he watched the liturgy of the Church.

. . . I would take communion at morning mass. The priest (a Spanish curé!) would take a host from the ciborium.
"What sauce do they steep in?" I wondered. The sauce was the unction of the priest's pale fingers. In order to separate the hosts and take only one, he manipulated them with an unctuous gesture, as if he were stirring a thick liquid in a golden vase. Now, as I knew that they were flakes of dry white dough, I was astonished. . . . I felt God—or, rather than Him, a sickening impression

[25]

of mystery—by means of a few evil and sordid details (arising from a childish imagination) of the Roman liturgy.

The first play written by Genet (the second published) was *Deathwatch* (*Haute surveillance*). First performed February 24, 1949, at the Théâtre des Mathurins in Paris, directed by Genet himself, it was published the same year by Gallimard. The American edition, following the acting version, incorporates revisions Genet made during rehearsals.

Deathwatch may be taken to depict that "inner prison," the "festivals" of which Genet had said he would write about after *The Thief's Journal*. "The entire play," he advises, "unfolds as in a dream." In the prison cell where all the action takes place, an overhead light, harsh and direct, falls upon the "violent" colors (white and black) of the prisoners' garb. Beneath its glare is played out an "ideal" fatality of criminals. The principal character, Green Eyes, is strongly reminiscent of Harcamone in *Miracle de la rose*. They are the same type: the convict sentenced to die (though Green Eyes may be sent to French Guiana instead) because he has murdered someone and who, because of his deed and his sentence, receives the fearful esteem of his fellow prisoners. Two of the latter, Maurice and Lefranc, together with Green Eyes, form a triangle, the inner dynamics of which provide the substance of the play. A fourth character, a Negro whose name is Snowball, affects the triangle but does not appear on stage.

Maurice and Lefranc look up to Green Eyes, who stands at the apex of the triangle, defining themselves with reference to his being and potency. By this, their relation to each other is also defined. A continual process of shifting alliances, influences, and compulsions reaches its climax when Maurice is murdered by Lefranc.

Maurice, who at seventeen is the youngest of the three, conceives of Green Eyes as "the best of men," lordly in his independence, one to whom others are unnecessary and who is therefore an absolute necessity to lesser men; slight creatures

[26]

like Maurice can attain to glory only as they are the devotees of the truly great ones. Before Green Eyes, Maurice is spiritually prostrate. One of Genet's accomplishments is to make the audience feel the quality of spiritual devotion in Maurice at the same time that he is shown as a mere sycophant and a queer.

Lefranc, who at twenty-three is the oldest of the three, also looks up to Green Eyes, but with a different attitude. He would like to replace him in his pre-eminent position. Or, since that is for the present impossible, he wants to become like him, receiving a similar adulaton and sharing his destiny as a murderer. This makes him, as it were, an angel in revolt. It makes him also a heterodox figure who introduces into the faith of Maurice an element of doubt and restiveness that Maurice's need of absolute devotion cannot accommodate. Lefranc tries to destroy Maurice's esteem for Green Eyes by telling him that Green Eyes has entered into some sort of alliance with Snowball, who dwells in another part of the prison. This not only makes Maurice jealous, but also causes him to doubt the indifference and independence of Green Eyes, which he had thought to be cardinal attributes of his "divinity." Upset by his doubt, Maurice begins to hate the unseen Snowball and the "tempter" Lefranc, while at the same time he begins to stand in awe of them; if either man should replace Green Eyes as the embodiment of power, Maurice would have to shift his allegiance because he needs to adore power wherever it is most fully manifest. Because of this double attitude he partly goads Lefranc into becoming his murderer.

Maurice has much in common, spiritually, with the Genet of *Miracle de la rose*, whose worship of Harcamone was deflected at the crucial moment, giving way to a carnal engagement with Divers whom he allowed to bugger him. This immersed Genet deeply in guilt. In *Deathwatch* that sexual act is replaced by murder, and the guilt is replaced by death.

As Harcamone was untouched by Genet's defection at the

hour of his agony, so Green Eyes, the "saintly" criminal with his feet in chains, is untouched by the death of Maurice. However, he gives Lefranc the full complement of his scorn. Green Eyes despises Lefranc not because he thinks murder an act to be scorned but for quite the opposite reason: it is so holy an act (that is, so taboo) that it should not be performed out of Lefranc's motivations, or indeed for any *reasons*. It must be purely the result of the murderer's destiny. Since Lefranc has tried to force the hand of destiny, to steal its glory as Prometheus stole the fire of heaven, his act of murder attains only to a psychological meaning. It lacks the ontological substance that belongs to Green Eyes' *acte gratuit*.

Green Eyes remains supreme at the end of the play as at its beginning. He is above the petty lives of the "others." It is discovered that he has, in fact, entered into some sort of alliance with Snowball and that he has received a visit from his wife. The triangle having been destroyed that was formed by the three on-stage characters, another may be formed among Green Eyes and the two off-stage characters. In spite of this, the independence of Green Eyes is maintained. It is an inalienable attribute and cannot be compromised by any transactions he may have with ordinary mortals. *Deathwatch* is Genet's dramatization of the apotheosis of the authentic murderer.

The Maids (*Les Bonnes*) is radically different from all Genet's previous work because its characters are females. However, Genet's original intention was that they should be played by boys in women's clothing. The play was commissioned by Louis Jouvet, who produced and directed it with a cast of three actresses at the Théâtre Athénée in Paris on April 17, 1947. As in *Deathwatch*, the action of *The Maids* rises from the dynamics of a triangular relationship. At the apex of this one we find Madame, who is the employer of the two maids. As in *Deathwatch*, the figure at the apex of the triangle is untouched by the jealousies of the other two characters, which in this play also lead to the murder of the one by the other. If Madame is unaffected by the emotions and rivalries of her two maids, however, she is by no means irrelevant to them. A powerful force, the greater and the more sublime because of her indifference, she is on stage for only a brief time; but during the rest of it she is a vivid presence-in-absence. She is an ideal reality. To say it more accurately, she represents an ideal reality and is thus a stronger force when present only to her servants' imaginations than when she appears in person.

When the play begins, the audience is unaware that Madame is absent. We see a lady at her toilet, dressed in her slip, choosing clothes for the evening. She gives abrupt, scornful orders to her maid, whom she calls Claire. Gradually we became aware that the relation of these two is not only that of employer and servant. There are certain erotic overtones. Perhaps the maid adores her mistress and accepts her imperiousness because it stimulates in her a certain masochistic pleasure. For her part, Madame seems sadistically to enjoy her cruelty toward the maid. We also become aware that something in the scene is false. The relation of mistress to servant is exaggerated. Perhaps the two are playing roles. Is their relation so intimate that they sometimes change parts? Is the maid really the mistress? Has she perhaps fallen in love with her own maid, whom she then orders to wear her clothes, make herself beautiful, and give orders so that Madame may be abased before her? If so, we are witnessing the secret rituals that lie behind a *scandale* of the type that sometimes ends violently and makes headlines in the newspapers. We may have heard that Genet got the idea for the play from a newspaper story.

Suddenly the scene is shattered. An alarm clock rings. The two figures, thrown into panic, drop their roles. We learn, to our astonishment, that *neither* of them is Madame. They are both her maids. The ringing of the alarm clock, which they

[29]

have set, means that Madame is about to return. They begin
to tidy up, to get rid of any misplaced articles that might
betray to her the game they play in her absence. They do this
poorly, leaving certain telltale signs. We discover also that
the dominant of the two, whose name is Solange, has been
pretending to be the weaker. It was she who was called Claire.
The real Claire had been playing Madame. The two maids
are sisters.

Both Claire and Solange adore Madame. At the same time,
they hate her, partly because she holds such power over them
and partly because each sister is jealous of the other. We are
presented with a closed, yet dynamic, system in which love
and hatred, jealousy, revenge, and desire for possession play
off against each other. The stability of the system depends on
its instability. We will surmise correctly if we suppose that the
system is doomed to self-destruction.

Madame has a male lover who is in jail. He was put there
by Solange, who gave certain information anonymously to
the police. He now telephones that he has been released on
bail. Madame returns. She is as haughty, as overbearing as in
the performance of her given earlier by Claire, though in her
own person this trait is not so "perfect" as in the imitation.
They have planned to kill her by putting poison in her tea.
The stated motive for this act is revenge. It will be an act
symbolizing the revolt of all maids, all servants and prisoners
against their superiors. The hidden motive, however, is to
stabilize the relation between Claire and Solange by removing
the one whom both desire. Furthermore, the plan is engineered
by Solange, who gets Claire to administer the poison. If the
plan were to succeed, Claire's guilt would place her forever
in Solange's power.

The plan goes awry. Madame, excited by the prospect of
seeing Monsieur again, refuses to drink her tea. She changes
her clothes and departs. In her absence, the maids return to their

[30]

original masquerade. Claire will again pretend to be Madame. Solange will be Claire and will bring her the cup of poisoned tea. The game has gone too far, however, to remain mere pretense. It must reach a climax. At first the death of Madame is rehearsed as if it took place off stage. It is not sufficient. Claire desires to give herself completely to Solange. "It would be too simple," she says, "to conspire with the wind, to make the night our accomplice. Solange, you will contain me within you." She reduces the scene to its symbolic essence: "We're alone in the world. Nothing exists but the altar where one of the two maids is about to immolate herself. . . . In prison no one will know that I'm with you, secretly."

Then occurs one of those magical transformations of which Genet is so fond and of which the play has already included more than one. Claire, the weaker of the two, reveals herself as the stronger. She virtually mesmerizes Solange, feeding her the right lines to say and the right gestures to perform. Claire-Madame sits in her chair and orders her tea (in French, *tilleul*, or lime-blossom tea). Solange-Claire brings the fatal cup. Claire drinks it: "And you've poured it into the best, the finest tea set." Solange faces the audience without moving, "her hands crossed as if held by handcuffs," while the curtain descends.

In a letter *à propos* of *The Maids*, written in 1954 to Jean-Jacques Pauvert, the publisher of the play, Genet complained that "even the finest Western plays" have "an air of masquerade and not of ceremony." By contrast, he declared, "the loftiest modern drama has been expressed daily for two thousand years in the sacrifice of the Mass." There can be little doubt that in *The Maids* Genet, although he said he wrote the play in boredom, has composed the best example of ritual theater known to modern drama. Its sense of form is so acute, its writing so lean, its series of *agons* so forcefully built, and its air of ceremonious fatality so heavy that one is driven, for a comparison, to speak of classical and neo-classic tragedy.

[31]

Oreste Pucciani has analyzed it in terms of a five-movement structure analogous to the five acts of French tragedy. He calls it, correctly, "a nearly perfect tragedy in the French tradition." Genet inverts classical tragedy, he notes, by turning its kings and queens into housemaids; but he observes that Genet's wit transforms these lowly creatures "into queens of a sort." "Genet," he declares, "is Racine turned inside out." One is indeed reminded of Phèdre and her fatal, compulsive desire.

One day a producer will be daring enough to implement Genet's original plan to have *The Maids* performed by male actors in women's clothing. Then an audience may experience more fully the sense of preposterous inevitability upon which the play is built. For *The Maids* is a work in which the arbitrary and the necessary coalesce. Both of these qualities, the arbitrary and the necessary, have been grounded by Genet in an ontology of evil, whereby the "lie" of theater and the destructiveness of absolute desire receive their justification in the superiority of evil and non-being over the good and the true. On such a basis there may be wit but not comedy, immolation but not triumph. Those who are damned by society are, according to Genet, also damned by God. But in that very fact is to be seen their attraction and their glory. Genet sees it as a limitation of God that He cannot experience damnation.

Two years after the first performance of *The Maids*, Genet published (1949) the scenario of a ballet called *'Adame Miroir*, music for which was composed by Darius Milhaud. I have not been able to discover any reference to performance. In *The Thief's Journal* Genet says that the idea for the ballet came to him from watching a friend trapped in a Palace of Mirrors at a fairground. "He was looking at the crowd in a rage, and they were looking at him and laughing. The manager of the booth was indifferent."

The Balcony (*Le Balcon*), published in 1956, was written sometime during the two preceding years. It was the first work written by Genet after he had gained a wide audience and achieved a literary reputation. It demonstrated that, although he could hardly surpass the near-perfect formalism of *The Maids*, his theater was capable of a vast expansion in scope with no loss—and some would say an increase—of power.

The first version of *The Balcony* had fifteen scenes. Later, Genet revised it, reducing the number of scenes to nine. The 1956 edition included a lithograph by Alberto Giacometti, who was to be the subject of an appreciative essay by Genet, *L'Atelier d'Alberto Giacometti* (1958). The second version was published in 1960. Notable productions were given in London in 1957, Berlin in 1959, New York and Amsterdam in 1960. Paris saw it in May, 1960, after the New York production. Since then it has been done in Upsala, Stockholm, Copenhagen, Oslo, and Helsinki. Rights to its production have been secured in Poland, Yugoslavia, Brazil, and other countries where fear of censorship has so far kept it from the stage.

The germ of the idea for *The Balcony* is to be noticed in *Querelle de Brest*, in which much of the action takes place in a brothel called La Féria, presided over by Madame Lysiane. To it come not only the sailors and the Chief of Police but also a variety of clients with peculiar tastes: the petty officer, loved by one of *"les filles"* called Carmen, who must be served *confiture;* the retired admiral who likes to walk around naked with a feather stuck in his rear and who clucks like a chicken while one of the girls chases him dressed as the farmer's wife; another who likes to be chained to the foot of the bed while he barks; and so on. Thinking of these, Madame Lysiane sometimes says: "Happily, my girls, there are vices; this permits those who are all fucked up to know love." Genet remarks: "She was good."

In the play, the name of the brothel is The Balcony, Madame

Lysiane becomes Irma, Carmen is retained as the name of one of the girls, and the Chief of Police is one of the main characters. The dramatis personae number twenty-eight. The play is much longer than either *Deathwatch* or *The Maids*, and the single set gives way to many.

As in *The Maids*, the play opens with a "game." We see a bishop, in miter and gilded cope, sitting in his chair. On his feet are the *cothurni* of the Greek tragic actor. His shoulders are extraordinarily broad, his whole figure frighteningly large. He opens the play with these words:

In truth, the mark of a prelate is not mildness or unction, but rather the most vigorous intelligence. Our heart is our undoing. We think we are master of our kindness; we are the slave of a serene laxity. In fact, it is something quite other than intelligence that is involved. . . . (*He hesitates.*) It may be cruelty. And beyond that cruelty—and through it—a skillful, vigorous heading towards Absence. Towards Death. . . .

To one side stands a Woman. We learn that the bishop has heard her confess six deadly sins and has granted her absolution. In the doorway is Irma, the Madame. The scene is a studio in her brothel, the "bishop" a customer, one of those who needs vices in order to know love, and the house has just provided this man who works for the gas company with the illusions he requires in order to satisfy his lust.

In the second scene we are in another studio. Like the first, it has a mirror which seems to reflect an unmade bed located, as it were, "in the first rows of the orchestra." A judge is punishing a thief who is a young girl. In the third scene we find a general putting his horse, who is a girl wearing a large tail, through its paces. In the fourth, a little old man in a dirty wig is whipped by a girl wearing leather boots and corselet. In the fifth we come to the elegant room of Irma, and the plot begins.

Madame Irma's brothel, a house of illusions, exists in the capital city of a regime beset by revolution. From outside the house one can hear occasional bursts of machine gun fire. To the house come the mock bishop, general, and judge—that is, nobodies who here become august personages—and also a real official, though a petty one, the Chief of Police, who is a friend of Irma. He is the principal link between the house and the real world outside it. A girl named Chantal has deserted the house and joined the forces of the revolution. The insurgents are the enemy. They intended to destroy The Balcony along with the Government, the Queen, and the Royal Palace.

The sixth scene takes place outside the brothel. It is set in an old café held by the revolutionists. Their campaign is faltering at the very moment it might succeed. In direct contrast to the house of illusions, the revolution has been conceived as a movement of reason and unadorned truth. The revolutionists want to destroy the symbols of royal authority, religion, and military power, which are the prototypes of Madame Irma's shadow versions, in order to institute the rule of pure reason. But the revolutionists are discovering that they cannot maintain the allegiance of their own followers on such a basis, for in the strain of battle the fighters are losing heart without an emotional symbol round which they may rally. It is proposed to turn Chantal, the former whore of The Balcony, into such a symbol. As one puts it, freedom is a fine thing, "but it would be even finer if freedom were a pretty girl with a warm voice." Roger, the leader of the revolution, eventually agrees, and Chantal sings. The revolution lives by adopting the "irrational" appeal of its opposition.

Meanwhile the Queen has perished, and her Envoy comes to The Balcony to enlist the aid of Irma. Without its symbols, the Government cannot live. Will Madame Irma appear before the crowds as the Queen, attended by her retinue including the "bishop," the "judge," and the "general"? She agrees, and a royal appearance is staged on the balcony of The Balcony. Suddenly Chantal appears there also. A shot is fired, she falls,

[35]

and the "General" and the "Queen" carry her away dead. The "royal" party makes a procession through the city, which we do not see, and the revolution is over. The false figures have come to power.

The new regime is led by eminences who share a certain quality: all have status without function, and they owe their position to this fact. Their images incite lust, and that is the sign of their "reality." But there is one among them, the Chief of Police, of whom this is not true. He is merely a functionary and not a symbol. Therefore he longs for someone to come to The Balcony desirous of "being" the Chief of Police. He also longs to have a monument erected in his honor in the shape of an enormous phallus and located at the center of a mausoleum. At last a customer comes to The Balcony to play the role of the Chief of Police in the new "mausoleum" studio. It is Roger, the leader of the defeated revolution, who goes into the studio and there castrates himself. The Chief of Police, overjoyed, descends into the mausoleum saying he will stay two thousand years. He has been translated from a functionary into a symbolic figure. Machine gun fire starts up again in the streets. Irma sends everyone except the Chief of Police home by the door leading into the alley. She turns out the lights and covers the furniture as at the end of a working day. Tomorrow will be another. To the audience, her other customers, she says: "You must go home now, where everything—you can be quite sure—will be even falser than here."

The major theme of *The Balcony* may be stated as follows. The "real" world is saved by the illusory one. Deprived of its symbolic head, the Queen, the "real" society is forced to turn to Irma, whose business is the manufacture of illusions needed to satisfy the lusts of men. Since her pretended queenship and her false bishop, judge, and general serve as well as the "real" ones they succeed, we are to draw the implication that society's "real" symbols of royalty, religion, justice, and power are themselves only the manufactured products of a Madame whom we may call Imagination. Like Irma, she is a mistress of lies. As such, she may be called Evil, yet society cannot exist without her. She stands, so to speak, between mankind and nothingness, but whether as protectress or as betrayer it is impossible to say. Her opposite is not the "normal" world but pure rationality. The latter is not constructive. It can mount revolutions and fire machine guns, but it cannot govern or inspire love, because it is pure function devoid of status.

The corollary of this theme, characteristic of the myth of perverse sexuality, is that the ultimate object of desire is death. All the performances in all the studios of The Balcony are modes of dying. The one called the mausoleum is the epitome of the others. The destiny of all the characters is succinctly stated in one of the Envoy's remarks about Irma: "The Queen attains her reality when she withdraws, absents herself, or dies."

Irma is Genet. As playwright, he is the mistress of these illusions, the theater his bordello, we his paying customers. The dying king is here the dying queen, who, like Irma in the last moments of the play, turns out the lights one by one. But this dying is perpetual. It will occur again tomorrow. The nothingness of death is clearly seen in this: dying is only an act to be performed over and over again, always and always the same. Even death is not real. There is no reality. That is why the ending of The Balcony is pure contrivance. In an unreal world there can be no logical or existential end.

"One evening," writes Genet, "an actor asked me to write a play for an all-black cast. But what exactly is a black? First of all, what's his color?" From this request and this question emerged Genet's next play, The Blacks (Les Nègres), subtitled "A Clown Show." It was produced at the Théâtre de Lutèce in Paris in October, 1959, to great acclaim. Roger Blin, who directed it, could not find thirteen professional Negro actors in

Paris, and so he chose a cast of amateurs, whom he rehearsed for two years before the play's opening. This indicates that *The Blacks* was written during or before 1957, soon after Genet finished *The Balcony*.

To ask what is the color of a black means two things: (1) Is a black man always black? and (2) What is blackness? Both of these questions are ontological in character. The first toys with the difference of appearance from reality. The second invites speculation as to the nature of blackness, not only as the color of some persons' skin, but also as a thing or quality in its own right. *The Blacks* is Genet's most ontological play, concerned even more than *The Balcony* with the question, what is real?

It is also the play which, among all of Genet's, is most easily read as social commentary. Such a reading, however, may be erroneous, for the relation of the play to the subject of racial justice is at most indirect. One should say that racial conflict provides the occasion for the play, while its subject is something else.

The work is a (black) masque given for the entertainment of the (white) audience. It opens with eight Negroes, dowdily dressed, dancing to strains of Mozart around a catafalque which contains, so we are told, the body of a murdered white woman. There is to be a trial. The judges, who sit on an upper stage, are five white persons—that is, Negroes wearing white masks. They represent a queen, her governor, a missionary, judge, and valet.

In the first part of the play, the "facts" of the murder are related piecemeal and with great imprecision. The victim seems to change from moment to moment, also the motive. She was an old beggar woman, or a rich young woman, or a shy virgin, or some other kind of white woman. He (they) killed her for her money, or after a rape, or because he was spurned by a black woman, or because it was easy, or just because there has to be a new victim every night. The murder-rape is re-enacted with a certain Mr. Diouf, "a curate at St. Anne's" and an apologist for compromise, playing the victim by donning the mask of a white girl. When he (she) is dead, he goes to heaven—that is, to the upper stage among the whites. From there he reports "that they lie or that they're mistaken. They're not white, but pink or yellowish." He decides that he has become a pink woman and says that he moves about "in a light emitted by our faces which they reflect from one to another."

The second part of the play is a contest of strength, black versus white. Coming down from its upper level, the "white court" goes on a safari. In the African jungle, black and white meet, on black territory. The spirit of blackness, represented by a sixty-year-old Negress named Mrs. Felicity Trollop Pardon, engages the white queen in a battle of words. Felicity envisions an all black world: "Milk will be black, sugar, rice, the sky, doves, hope, will be black." Her long set speech on this theme is of remarkable rhetoric and reminds one of Melville's chapter on whiteness in *Moby Dick*. The language of the play reminds one also of Renaissance extravagances and the verbal displays of the Jacobean dramatists, whom Genet read while in prison. It is likely that he was directly influenced by John Webster.

The play ends as it began. The Negroes gather once more around the catafalque. They pull the sheet from it, revealing only a couple of the queen's chairs. They laugh wildly, then resume the Mozart dance. The show is over. Meanwhile, however, a real murder has been committed off stage.

The ritual of the play has several meanings. On the surface of it, the blacks, who represent all classes of persons who are victimized by those in power, put on a "clown show" which, like a minstrel, depicts the blacks as the white persons believe them to be—savage, stupid, erotic, given to aping white man-

[39]

ners. Beneath the surface, however, there lies a ritual of revenge. If whites blame Negroes for murders they have not committed (the mock trial of the imaginary murderer of a non-existent white woman), nevertheless Negroes are willing and able to revenge themselves by real murders, which they keep hidden (like the one off stage). Furthermore, the ritual in which, for the benefit of the white audience, the Negroes mock themselves, contains also a bitter mockery of the whites. The very servility of the Negroes, since it is a pose, contains great scorn. An audience watching *The Blacks* finds itself assaulted and ridiculed, drawn into the ritual only to be betrayed and ritually slain as the "white court" is slain in the jungle.

Bernard Frechtman, Genet's very able translator, has said that *The Blacks* is about power. That is true, but more fundamentally it is about energy, of which power is a principal manifestation. The play's obsession with energy shows that Genet has shifted considerably from *The Balcony*. There the dialectic was between illusion and nothingness, with the implication that at the bottom of all things there is nothing. In *The Blacks* the dialectic is between formless energy and its organization into forms of ritual and power. The play is continually dissolving and then coming again into shape. All its depictions are of epiphenomena. Yet when these disappear we are not plunged into nothingness. Instead we descend into a primordial flux of energy out of which new rituals, oppressions, and revenges are born.

Perhaps Genet is suggesting that our conscious life, our political and social "realities," our exercise of power, our religions and systems of ideas, even our color and our sex, are all manifestations of a ceaseless energy that casts up in its irrational way the phenomena which we call, in the aggregate, life. Perhaps the vast quantities of psychic energy that *The Blacks* releases in its audience is the result not only of its being attacked but also of Genet's having shattered the "atoms" of normal consciousness, letting loose the energies of which they are composed. One is fascinated by the potential of energy thus released even while he may be terrified by the prospect of its unpredictable fallout.

However that may be, it is clear that the pertinence *The Blacks* has to "the racial problem" is not that of an advocate of the "cause" of Negroes, let alone that of one who pleads for justice. Genet's play has almost nothing in common with the angry outbursts of a James Baldwin or a LeRoi Jones and even less with liberal pleas such as were written by the late Lorraine Hansberry. What he does show is that the relation of oppressor to oppressed is a relation containing enormous energies and that when this unstable relation is changed the energies pour out as violence directed not only against persons but also against preconceived forms of consciousness. One could draw the conclusion that it would be safest to preserve the *status quo* in the hope of protecting society against the release of such energies, but Genet suggests that this is not possible.

In *The Blacks* the myths of the dying king and of perverse sexuality are subordinated to a new preoccupation. Narcissism, compulsive attraction to form, and ontological nihilism give way to a kind of ontological affirmation. Outside the self's hall of mirrors there is "something." We may call it energy. However wild and terrifying, it is "there"; and it has power not only to destroy but also to create. *The Blacks* is Genet's emergence from prison.

The first performance of *The Screens* (*Les Paravents*) took place in West Berlin in June, 1961. Roger Blin, who had spent a month helping Genet in Italy to polish the script, and who wanted to direct it in Paris, told Bettina Knapp in an interview published in 1963, "It cannot be produced in Paris. It's too dangerous since it deals with the Algerian War. The Arabs

[41]

versus the French on stage. Why we would all be bombed!" The play was staged in 1962 in Vienna and in 1964 in Stockholm. A London production directed by Peter Brook in 1964 included only the first half of the play and was shown only to invited audiences. The work at last reached Paris, without bombs, on April 21, 1966, when Jean-Louis Barrault presented it at the state-subsidized Théâtre de France. Roger Blin directed a cast of sixty that included Maria Casares, Madeleine Renaud, and M. Barrault. *The New York Times* reported that, instead of causing the national scandal that some had predicted, the play emerged "as an unequivocal theatrical triumph, one of the major achievements of the French Theater since World War II."

The Screens, which is the last work Genet has written, is of a larger scope than any of his earlier plays. It has over forty characters. The stage directions say that it should be put on in an open-air theater. The last of its seventeen scenes employs nine screens, arranged on three separate levels, representing seven different localities, among them a prison, a village square, and a region of the dead. Large screens, "each about ten feet high," are used as the principal part of the set throughout the play, to which they have given their name. They are almost like part of the dramatis personae. Each is to be mounted on rubber-tired wheels so as to roll silently on a carpet when moved by a stagehand, whom the screen will hide. The screens are frequently used as canvases on which the characters draw objects to identify the locale of the action or to suggest important events that are taking place. The imaginative extravagance of this device as Genet employs it is unmatched in the modern theater. The whole work is lavish in conception. It is a spectacle, though utterly unlike the sumptuous spectacles most often found in the commercial theater.

In *The Screens* Genet has moved as far as possible from the prison world of *Miracle de la rose* and *Deathwatch*. *The Maids* had left the prison setting behind but had re-created the prison ethos among three members of a household. *The Balcony* had shown a great enlargement of scope but had insisted that men are confined within a system of illusions that reflect each other like so many mirrors. Its action had been placed in a brothel in a city. *The Blacks*, which seems to spread over an entire continent, had rejected the psychology of the prison world entirely, positing a genuine, non-illusory reality outside the confines of ritualized existence. Now in *The Screens* Genet made the action, while ostensibly occuring in war-torn Algeria, seem to take place in the vastness of the universe.

The subject of this remarkable play is the coincidence of absolute freedom with absolute dejection. Its villains are the French *colons* and the French military, who are full of narcissistic pride and have no existence save in their self-images. While they strut and murder and seek the beauty of privileged cruelty, the play's heart descends with the lowly Arabs into poverty, moral abjection, ugliness, and the end of all pretense. No doubt the Arabs are romanticized by being made, in their humiliation, so superior to their oppressors, but the play is not political. It is concerned with a moral reality, the name of which is *ascesis*.

The coincidence of freedom and dejection had been present in Genet's writing from the first, but it had always been presented with a certain irony, as if Genet did not quite believe it, as if, seeing its irony, he loved it only as a beautiful fiction. In *The Screens* he presents it instead as a true paradox. The play, in spite of its massiveness, soars and wheels like some giant bird. It is Genet's most sordid play, a work one has to say is conceived in filth, and at the same time it is exalted, a mystic vision of the spiritual triumph of the dispossessed. Imbued with great love, it is Genet's *Inferno* and *Paradiso* in one.

All the works of Genet until *The Blacks* are predicated upon a great, even a diabolic, falsehood. I have called it the myth of the dying king or the myth of perverse sexuality. What that means is that Genet, who had pledged himself as a child to the pursuit of evil, created dazzling and sometimes beautiful works out of the insistence that evil is superior to good because it is nothingness expressed as pure form. Such a notion is perverse. It contains only the illusion of logic, and it can be maintained only by the sheer exercise of the will. Precisely this was its appeal to Genet, and to Sartre, who perceived it in him. The mock death of the mock king, who is really a queen of exquisite, though self-inflicted, agony, contained superb possibilities for verbal and theatrical constructs. It led to a verbal "victory." The books and the early plays contained much genuine passion, which Genet betrayed, in both senses of the word. He revealed it and at the same time turned it into charade. This performance was capable of seducing some readers (so Genet seems to have hoped) into a love of evil. Others it repulsed. Some, not seduced, were thrilled by its diabolism. The most perceptive took it as an unparalleled expression of the philosophical, aesthetic, and moral perversity of which man is capable. Genet wrote in artistic form a phenomenology of sin. The miracle was that he was so acutely aware of what he was doing.

Then history seems to have intervened. One cannot know why it did so with a positive moral effect when it had not done so earlier in the period of Naziism. In any case, the struggle of black men to free themselves from centuries of indignity and the struggle of North African Arabs to end colonial domination provided Genet in *The Blacks* and *The Screens* with material that not only appealed to his imagination but seems also to have modified his moral and ontological understandings. In neither play did Genet espouse a social cause. In both the relation to political and historical matters is tangential. Yet tangents are not always to be despised, and Genet's brush with recent history seems to have occasioned in him a change. It seems to have enabled him to begin to conceive of a reality transcending human imagination, and this not merely the "God" whom he had met in ritual and whom he had to oppose, but something too real to be named yet dimly sensed as authentic and true.

To read as many as two of Genet's works is to realize that they are interdependent. To read them all is to become aware that their unity, above and beyond matters of style, tone, and motif, is the unity of a moral—yes, a saintly—enterprise of extraordinary intensity. They record the pilgrimage of a criminal-saint who went out from his prison-monastery. Taking at first its images and rituals with him, he later discarded them because they were too rich and too confining. He touched instead the real, which he could not define, but which he could at last believe is there.

BIBLIOGRAPHY

NOTE: *English translations (mentioned in parentheses) are by Bernard Frechtman unless otherwise noted.*

I. THE WORKS OF JEAN GENET

'Adame Miroir. Ballet in collaboration with Mlle. Jeanine Charrat, music by Darius Milhaud. Paris, Paul Morihien, 1949.

L'Atelier d'Alberto Giacometti. Les Bonnes, suivi d'une lettre de l'auteur. L'Enfant criminel. Le Funambule. Décines, Isère, L'Arbalète, 1958. *L'Atelier* . . . reprinted 1963 with a drawing by the author and photos by Ernest Scheidegger.

Le Balcon. With a lithograph by Alberto Giacometti. Décines, Isère, L'Arbalète, 1956. 2nd ed., 1962. (The Balcony. New York, Grove Press, 1958; revised, 1960. London, Faber and Faber, 1958.)

Les Beaux gars. Twenty-seven drawings by Jean Boullet. Nice, Société d'Imprimerie Mediterranéenne, 1951.

Les Bonnes. Décines, Isère, L'Arbalète, no. 12, 1948. 2nd ed. (Sceaux, Jean-Jacques Pauvert, 1954) includes the first and the revised versions, preceded by a letter of Genet. Original version reprinted in L'Atelier d'Alberto Giacometti, 1958. New edition, Les Bonnes, et comment jouer Les Bonnes: Décines, Isère, L'Arbalète, 1963. (The Maids. Preface by Jean-Paul Sartre. New York, Grove Press, 1954.)

Chants secrets. With a lithograph by Émile Picq. Contains Le Condamné à mort and Marche funèbre. Lyons, L'Arbalète, 1945.

Haute surveillance. Paris, Gallimard, 1949. (The Maids/Death-watch. New York, Grove Press, 1954; revised, 1962. London, Faber & Faber, 1961.)

Journal du voleur. Paris, Gallimard, 1949. (The Thief's Journal. Paris, Olympia Press, 1954. With a foreword by Jean-Paul Sartre. New York, Grove Press, 1964; Bantam Books, 1965.)

Miracle de la rose. Lyons, L'Arbalète, 1946. Second edition, Décines, Isère, L'Arbalète, 1957. (Miracle of the Rose. London, Anthony Blond, Ltd., 1965. New York, Grove Press, 1966.)

Les Nègres; clownerie. With a cover designed by Genet. Décines, Isère, L'Arbalète, 1958. Second edition, 1960, illustrated with Ernest Scheidegger's 33 photographs of the Paris performance, introductory note by Genet. 1963 edition, also with photos by E. Scheidegger, is entitled Pour jouer les "Nègres," clownerie. (The Blacks, a Clown Show. New York, Grove Press, 1960. London, Faber & Faber, 1960.)

"A Note on Theatre." Tulane Drama Review, VII, 3 (Spring 1963), 37–41. This is the "letter" that precedes the 1954 edition of the two versions of Les Bonnes.

Notre-Dame-des-Fleurs. Fragment: Revue l'Arbalète, no. 8, 1944. Complete: Monte Carlo, n.p., 1944. 2nd ed.: Décines, Isère, L'Arbalète, 1948. (The Gutter in the Sky. Trans. unknown. Philadelphia, A. Levy, 1955. Our Lady of the Flowers. Trans. Bernard Frechtman. Intro. by Jean-Paul Sartre. New York, Grove Press, 1963; Bantam Books, 1964; Modern Library, 1965. London, Anthony Blond, Ltd., 1964.)

Oeuvres complètes.
Vol. I. See "Sartre, Jean-Paul" under "Critical Works and Commentary."
Vol II. Paris, Gallimard, 1951. Contains Notre-Dame-des-Fleurs, Le Condamné à mort, Miracle de la rose, Un Chant d'amour.
Vol. III. Paris, Gallimard, 1953. Contains Pompes funèbres, Le Pêcheur du Suquet, Querelle de Brest.

Les Paravents. Décines, Isère, L'Arbalète, 1961. (The Screens. London, Faber & Faber, 1963. New York, Grove Press, 1963.)

Poèmes. With 21 photographs by Genet. Lyons, L'Arbalète, 1948. Second edition: Décines, Isère, L'Arbalète, 1962.

Pompes funèbres. Bikini (?), 1947. Revised and corrected ed., 1948.

Querelle de Brest. Clandestine ed., n.p., n.d. Ed. with 29 original lithographs (by Jean Cocteau?), Milan: n.p., 1947. New ed., n.p., 1947.

"To a Would-Be Producer." *Tulane Drama Review*, VII, 3 (Spring 1963), 80–81. Trans. of a letter sent by Genet in 1961 to Jerzy Lisowski refusing permission to do Les Nègres in Poland.

II. CRITICAL WORKS AND COMMENTARY

Abel, Lionel. Metatheatre. New York, Hill & Wang, 1963. See "Genet and Metatheatre," pp. 76–83.

Bataille, Georges. La Littérature et le mal. Paris, Gallimard, 1957. See "Genet," pp. 185–226.

Brustein, Robert. The Theatre of Revolt. Boston, Little, Brown, 1964. See ch. IX, "Antonine Artaud and Jean Genet," pp. 361–411.

Cismaru, Alfred. "The Antitheism of Jean Genet." *Antioch Review*, XXIV, 3 (Fall 1964), 387–401.

Clark, Eleanor. "The World of Jean Genet." *Partisan Review*, 16 (April 1949), 442–8.

Dort, Bernard. "Le Jeu de Genet." *Les Temps Modernes*, XV, 171 (June 1960), 1875–84.

Driver, Tom F. Review of *The Thief's Journal*. *New York Times Book Review*, Nov. 15, 1964, p. 4.

Driver, Tom F. "Spiritual Diabolism of Jean Genet." *Christian Century*, LXXX (Nov. 20, 1963), 1433–35.

Ehrmann, Jacques. "Genet's Dramatic Metamorphosis: from Appearance to Freedom." *Yale French Studies*, XXIX (Spring–Summer 1962), 33–42.

Esslin, Martin. The Theatre of the Absurd. New York, Doubleday & Co. (Anchor Books), 1961. See ch. IV, pp. 140–167.

Fowlie, Wallace. "The New French Theatre: Artaud, Beckett, Genet, Ionesco." *Sewanee Review*, LXVII, 4 (Fall 1959), 643–57.

Goldman, Lucien. "Une Pièce réaliste: 'Le Balcon' de Genet." *Les Temps Modernes*, XV, 171 (June 1960), 1885–96.

Grossvogel, David I. *Four Playwrights and a Postscript: Brecht, Ionesco, Beckett, Genet*. Ithaca, Cornell University Press, 1963.

Heist, Walter. "Die Faschistische Komponente: Randbemerkungen zum Werk von Jean Genet." *Frankfurter Hefte*, XVII (January 1962), 29–39.

McMahon, Joseph H. The Imagination of Jean Genet. New Haven, Yale University Press, 1963.

Nelson, Benjamin. "*The Balcony* and Parisian Existentialism." *Tulane Drama Review*, VII, 3 (Spring 1963), 60–79.

[47]

Pronko, Leonard C. "Jean Genet's *Les Paravents.*" *L'Esprit Créatur* (Minneapolis), II, 4 (Winter 1962), 181–88.

Pucciani, Oreste F. "Tragedy, Genet and *The Maids.*" *Tulane Drama Review*, VII, 3 (Spring 1963), 42–59.

Sartre, Jean-Paul. Saint Genet, comédien et martyr. Vol. I of Genet, Oeuvres complètes. Paris, Gallimard, 1952. (*Saint Genet, Actor and Martyr.* New York, George Braziller, 1963. New York, Mentor Books, 1964.)

Svendson, J. M. "Corydon Revisited: a Reminder on Genet." *Tulane Drama Review*, VII, 3 (Spring 1963), 98–110.

Taubes, Susan. "The White Mask Falls." *Tulane Drama Review*, VII, 3 (Spring 1963), 85–92.

Wellwarth, George E. The Theater of Protest and Paradox. New York, New York University Press, 1964. See "Jean Genet: the Theater of Illusion and Disillusion," pp. 113–33.

COLUMBIA ESSAYS ON MODERN WRITERS

EDITOR: William York Tindall
ADVISORY EDITORS:
Jacques Barzun, W.T.H. Jackson,
Joseph A. Mazzeo, Justin O'Brien

 1 *Albert Camus*, by Germaine Brée
 2 *William Golding*, by Samuel Hynes
 3 *Hermann Broch*, by Theodore Ziolkowski
 4 *Samuel Beckett*, by William York Tindall
 5 *Constantine Cavafy*, by Peter Bien
 6 *Lawrence Durrell*, by John Unterecker
 7 *Eugène Ionesco*, by Leonard C. Pronko
 8 *C. P. Snow*, by Robert Gorham Davis
 9 *Michel Butor*, by Leon S. Roudiez
10 *E. M. Forster*, by Harry T. Moore
11 *Alain Robbe-Grillet*, by Bruce Morrissette
12 *John Millington Synge*, by Denis Johnston
13 *Louis-Ferdinand Céline*, by David Hayman
14 *Raymond Queneau*, by Jacques Guicharnaud
15 *W. B. Yeats*, by William York Tindall
16 *Joyce Cary*, by William Van O'Connor
17 *Graham Greene*, by David Lodge
18 *Virginia Woolf*, by Carl Woodring
19 *Franz Kafka*, by Walter H. Sokel
20 *Jean Genet*, by Tom F. Driver
21 *Gerard Manley Hopkins*, by Francis Noel Lees
22 *Hermann Hesse*, by Theodore Ziolkowski

Each pamphlet, 65 cents. Orders accepted only for 6 or m[
pamphlets, same or assorted titles.

Distributed in the United Kingdom and in Europe by
Columbia University Press, Ltd., 6a Bedford Square, London W.[
U.K. price: 5s net

Order from your bookseller or from
COLUMBIA UNIVERSITY PRESS
2960 Broadway, New York, NY 10027